A LEVEL FOR EVERY READER

This book is a part of an exciting four-level reading series to support children in developing the habit of reading widely for both pleasure and information. Each book is designed to develop a child's reading skills, fluency, grammar awareness, and comprehension in order to build confidence and enjoyment when reading.

Ready for a Level 1 (Learning to Read) book

A child should:

- be familiar with most letters and sounds.
- understand how to blend sounds together to make words.
- have an awareness of syllables and rhyming sounds.

A valuable and shared reading experience

For many children, learning to read requires much effort, but adult participation can make reading both fun and easier. Here are a few tips on how to use this book with an early reader:

Check out the contents together:

- tell the child the book title and talk about what the book might be about.
- read about the book on the back cover and talk about the contents page to help heighten interest and expectation.
- chat about the pictures on each page.
- discuss new or difficult words.

Support the reader:

- give the book to the young reader to turn the pages.
- if the book seems too hard, support the child by sharing the reading task.

Talk at the end of each page:

- ask questions about the text and the meaning of the words used—this helps develop comprehension skills.
- read the quiz at the end of the book and encourage the reader to answer the questions, if necessary, by turning back to the relevant pages to find the answers.

Series consultant, Dr. Linda Gambrell, Distinguished Professor of Education at Clemson University, has served as President of the National Reading Conference, the College Reading Association, and the International Reading Association.

DK Penguin Random House

For Dorling Kindersley
Senior Editor Elizabeth Dowsett
Managing Art Editor Ron Stobbart
Publishing Manager Catherine Saunders
Art Director Lisa Lanzarini
Associate Publisher Simon Beecroft
Category Publisher Alex Allan
Production Editor Marc Staples
Production Controller Rita Sinha

For Lucasfilm
Executive Editor J. W. Rinzler
Art Director Troy Alders
Keeper of the Holocron Leland Chee
Director of Publishing Carol Roeder

Reading Consultant Dr. Linda Gambrell

Designed and edited by Tall Tree Ltd
Designer Darren Jordan
Editor Jon Richards

First published in the United States in 2011
by DK Publishing
1450 Broadway, Suite 801, New York, NY 10018

20 21 22 10 9 8 7 6
012 – 177103 – Jan/2011

A catalog record for this book is available
from the Library of Congress.

ISBN: 978-0-7566-7128-0 (Paperback)
ISBN: 978-0-7566-7129-7 (Hardback)

Printed in China

For the curious

www.dk.com

www.starwars.com

STAR WARS

TATOOINE ADVENTURES

Written by Clare Hibbert

Come and explore the planet Tatooine (TA-TOO-EEN) and meet the many different creatures that live here.

This dry, desert world is far away, on the edge of the galaxy.

Two suns keep the planet very hot.

Planet

This is Anakin Skywalker.

He is a slave who lives on Tatooine.

He belongs to a junk merchant called Watto.

Watto

Anakin fixes
machines for
Watto.

He builds a
droid called
C-3PO.

C-3PO will
be covered in
golden metal.

Droid

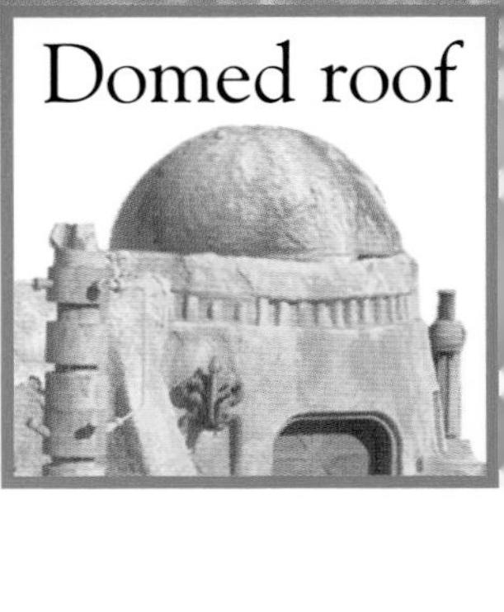

Anakin lives in a busy city called Mos Espa.

Many of the buildings in Mos Espa have domed roofs.

The biggest building is the Grand Arena.

It has a famous racetrack.

Podracing is the most popular sport on Tatooine.

The Podracers go super-fast.

Anakin is racing. Go, Anakin, go! Some of the other creatures in the Podrace cheat, but they can't beat Anakin!

Sand People live on Tatooine.
They are also called Tusken Raiders.

They live in small camps far out in the desert.

The Sand People are fierce fighters.

Tusken Raiders ride across the sand dunes on big hairy beasts called banthas.

Banthas have shaggy coats and long, curled horns.

They can survive for weeks without water.

These little aliens are Jawas. They are scavengers who buy and sell things.

Jawas wear hooded brown cloaks. All you can see are their eyes that glow orange or yellow.

Scavenger

Wow! Look at this old hunk.
It's called a sandcrawler.

Jawas live inside sandcrawlers.
They drive them across the desert.

They stop to pick up scrap metal and machine parts to fix and sell.

The Jawas have found a droid called R2-D2.

Anakin has a son called Luke.
Luke grows up on Tatooine.
He is raised by the Lars family.
They have a moisture farm.
They collect water from the air.

Owen Lars

The Lars live in
the desert.
The nearest city is
Mos Eisley
(MOSS IZE-LEE).

Moisture farm

This bar is in Mos Eisley.
It is full of troublemakers.

Luke is here to find someone to fly him and his friends to the planet Alderaan.

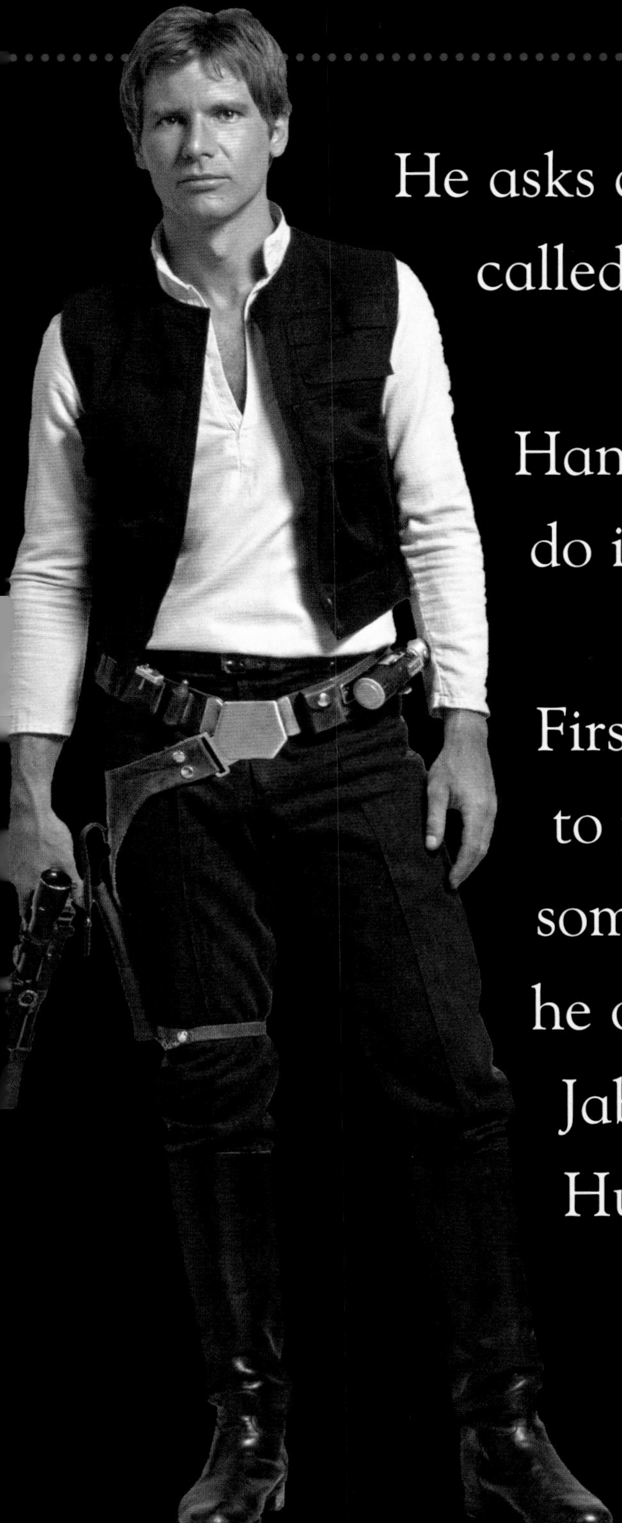

He asks a pilot
called Han Solo.

Han Solo will
do it.

First he needs
to pay back
some money
he owes to
Jabba the
Hutt.

Is this a giant slug?
No, it's Jabba the Hutt.
He's the most powerful being on Tatooine.

Jabba is a crime lord.
He loves to make bets and gamble money.
He has a terrible temper.

Jabba is protected by green-skinned guards.

They are strong but not very smart.

The guards come from a planet called Gamorr. They have horns, tusks, and short, pig-like snouts.

Look out, C-3PO! He's behind you!

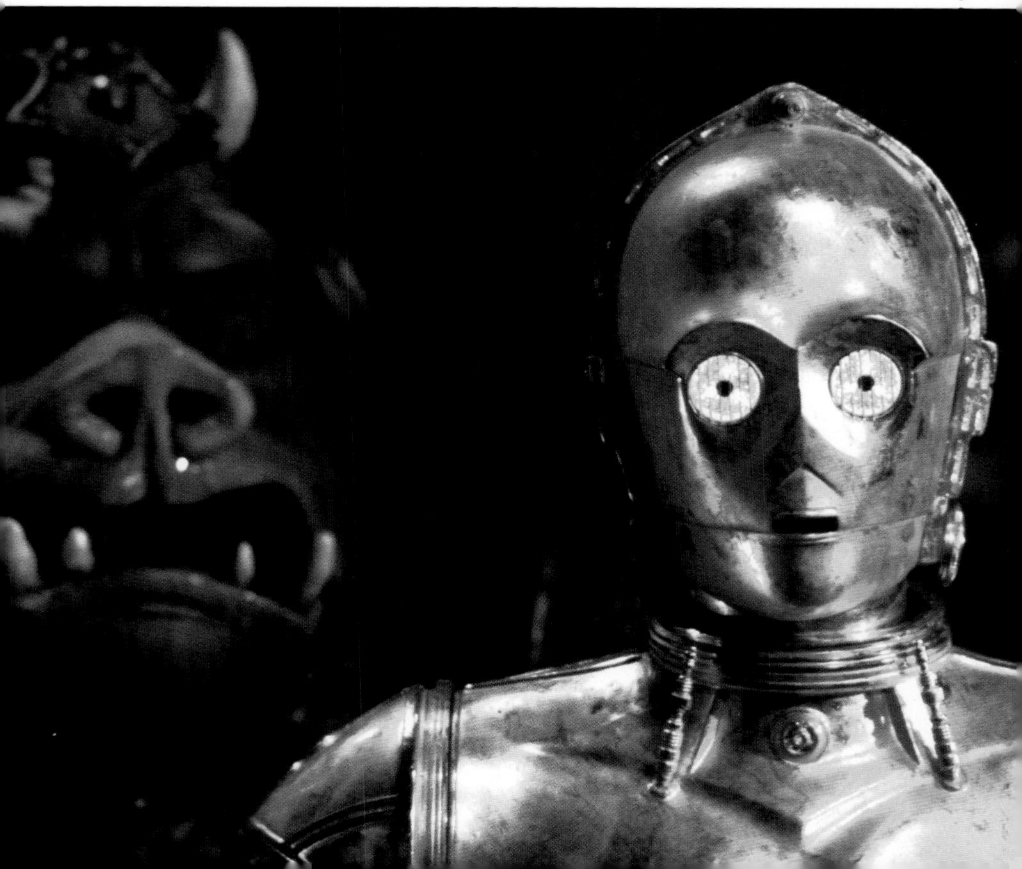

Yikes!
This monster is Jabba's pet.
It is a rancor and it lives in a giant pit under the floor.

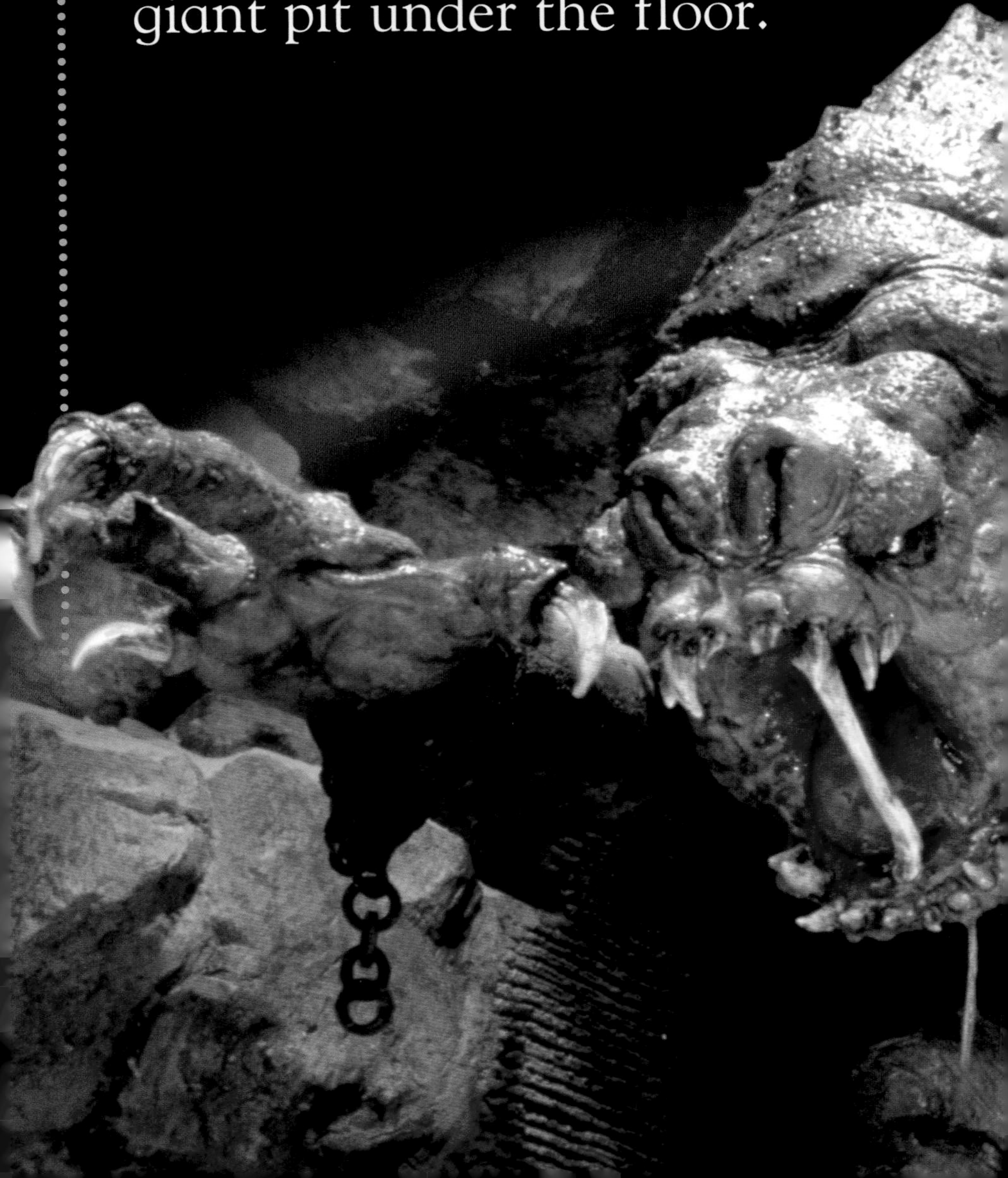

Uh oh!
Sometimes Jabba throws people into the pit.
The rancor gobbles them up.

Fire! Fire!
Jabba the Hutt's sail barge has been blasted by a laser cannon.
It's the end for you, Jabba.

You won't be cruising across the planet in this barge again. Looks like it's time for us to leave Tatooine!

Glossary

Droid
a robot

Domed roof
a roof that is shaped like half a ball

Moisture farm
a place where people collect water from the air

Planet
a ball of rock and gas that orbits around a star

Scavenger
someone who collects scrap and bits of metal